# TREEHOUSES

David Larkin
after E.H. Shepard

# TREE HOUSES

## The Art and Craft of Living Out on a Limb

Peter Nelson

EDITED AND DESIGNED BY DAVID LARKIN

PRINCIPAL PHOTOGRAPHY BY PAUL ROCHELEAU

WITH DRAWINGS BY ROYAL BARRY WILLS AND CHARLES H. CROMBIE

Houghton Mifflin Company

Boston  New York  1994

For information about permission
to reproduce selections from this book,
write to Permissions, Houghton Mifflin Company,
215 Park Avenue South,
New York, New York 10003

Library of Congress Cataloging-in-Publication Data
Nelson, Peter
Treehouses / by Peter Nelson; principal photography by
Paul Rocheleau.
p.   cm.
"A David Larkin book."
ISBN 0-395-62950-0 (cloth). ISBN 0-395-62949-7
(paper)
1. Treehouses. I. Title.
TH4890.N45     1994
728'.9--dc20
93-32568
CIP

Printed in Italy

SFE 10 9 8 7 6 5 4 3 2 1

Color separation by Sfera - Milan
Printed and bound by Sfera/Garzanti - Milan

One cold winter when I was in high school, my best friend and I spent most of our spare time drawing up elaborate plans for the treehouse we were going to build when spring came. Unfortunately, by the time spring finally arrived we had moved on to a plan to raft down the Amazon, and the treehouse never got built. Over the years I became a professional builder, of boats and houses (ground houses, as I think of them now), but I never did get around to constructing a treehouse, though I dreamed of it often.

Then one day I got a letter from my old friend reminding me of our great plans, and I decided it was finally time to turn my dreams into wood. In my backyard I had a beautiful old cottonwood tree about four feet thick at the base. Apart from wreaking havoc on the foundation of my house, it was a nice shade tree, and in fact it was one of the reasons I bought the house. After staring at the tree for a long time, I decided that it wanted a half-suspended treehouse. So I built a six-by-eight-foot platform, six feet off the ground, with one end bolted to the trunk of the cottonwood and the other suspended from a $1/2$-inch cable that hung from the upper branches of the tree. On top of the platform I constructed a tiny house using basic two-by-four framing, but with a few embellishments such as a brick fireplace and chimney.

I learned a lot building that first treehouse. I knew that in ordinary construction, most jobs take twice as long as the time you budget for them, but I discovered that with treehouses the ratio is more like three or four to one. I also discovered that building a treehouse is an all-engrossing project. You lose interest in normal daily pursuits and find yourself working late into the night, often high in a tree with dangerous power tools, at great risk to personal health and relationships. I learned that while spontaneity and improvisation are the essence of treehouse construction, a certain amount of planning is helpful, especially on the structural side. For example, the fireplace I impulsively added turned out not to be such a good idea. As I was writing this book, I got a letter from the people who had bought my old house and had turned the treehouse into a sauna. They told me how they had been awakened one night by a loud crash, and when they rushed outside they found that the brick chimney had collapsed, bringing the treehouse down with it.

That first treehouse only whetted my appetite, and since then I have built a half dozen more, including the house that is the centerpiece of this book. I have also gotten in the habit of seeking out treehouses and treehouse builders wherever I travel, and as I collected their stories and passed them along to others, I discovered that a fascination with treehouses is an almost universal human phenomenon. "You ought to write a book," people said. And so I did.

# HISTORY

What is it about a treehouse that causes almost everyone who sees it to pause, take a closer look, and smile? Our affection for treehouses may be inborn, for our ancestors lived in trees, and perhaps in some primal memory we still think of them as home. Or the smile may be evoked by more immediate memories: a treehouse built in childhood, or one read about in a favorite book— *Swiss Family Robinson, Tarzan, Winnie the Pooh.* Or a treehouse may represent escape: from adults or adulthood, from duties and responsibilities, from an earthbound perspective. If we can't fly with the birds, at least we can nest with them.

Whatever the reason, people have long built houses in trees, sometimes for protection from enemies or floods, but more often simply for pleasure. The Roman Emperor Caligula held banquets in the branches of an enormous plane tree, and during the Italian Renaissance the Medici vied to see who could build the grandest treehouse. Cosimo furnished his treehouse at Villa Castello with a marble table and plumbing, but his son Francesco trumped him with a treehouse that had not only a marble table but marble benches, a fountain, and two staircases. Built in the boughs of a Holm oak, like his father's house, Francesco's treehouse was called *La Fonte delle Rovere,* or "the fountain of oak."

The Medici treehouses are mentioned by many travelers, including Montaigne, who visited them in 1580, and are illustrated in engravings of the time. Treehouses often appear in European art of the 1500s and 1600s, particularly the works of Hieronymus Bosch and Pieter Brueghel, suggesting the popularity of treehouses in the Netherlands then. In Tudor England treehouses were also common, and one of the most remarkable was a three-story house at Cobham Hall in Kent. It was built in an enormous linden tree, with the branches bent downward to create three enclosed arbors eight feet high, one on top of the other. The middle arbor, which served as banquet hall, could hold over 50 people, and Queen Elizabeth I once attended a dinner there.

The Medici and Cobham Hall treehouses are long gone, but two notable early European treehouses still survive. One is the 16th-century treehouse at Pitchford Hall, shown below. The other is not actually a house at all, but a tree church that has been in continuous use for over 800 years. Located in the town of Allouville-Bellefosse, Normandy, it consists of two chapels, one above the other, in the hollow center of a great oak. The lower chapel, decorated with ornate wood carvings of the Madonna, can hold only a few people but is the focal point of village celebrations. The upper chapel, even smaller, is reached by a circular wooden staircase. A sign above the entrance to the lower chapel reads: "Be warned that it is forbidden, under the pain of a fine, to remove the bark or branches of the oak, or the leaves. Civil action will be taken against those who do so." Still, the tree has deteriorated with age. Its main branches have been reinforced with cables, and large cracks have been covered with roofs to keep the water out. The little roofs make the tree look as if it is inhabited by elves.

This half-timbered treehouse in an English linden is over 300 years old. In the late 1700s, the house was plastered on the outside and the interior was remodeled with elaborate friezes and moldings. Queen Victoria visited the house in 1832, when she was 13. After a gale almost destroyed the tree and the house in 1977, columns were built under the house, and the tree limbs were braced with steel cables. The exterior was also restored to its original appearance.

Historically, treehouses seem to have been most common in the South Pacific and Southeast Asia. When Captain Cook sailed into Tasmania in the late 1700s, he discovered the inhabitants living in the treetops, and some South Pacific Islanders lived in thatched nests in the trees, transporting themselves up and down in large baskets. The etching at left shows a treehouse observation post in the Malay archipelago.

In inland New Guinea, treehouses called *dobbos* were used as fortresses. When a village was under attack, the people would climb into the treehouses and pull the ladders up behind them. If the attackers attempted to chop down the tree, they would be pelted with stones and spears from above. Treehouses were also built as resting places for the dead in New Guinea.

This 1879 etching shows treehouses and polehouses
built on the banks of a river on the island of
Mindanao in the Philippines, presumably to avoid
flooding.

Probably the most famous treehouse in literature is the one in *Swiss Family Robinson,* a book by Johann Wyss that was first published in 1813. When their ship broke apart on a reef near New Guinea, the Robinsons, a mother, father, and four sons, climbed into tubs and rowed to a nearby island, their two dogs swimming along beside them. To protect themselves against wild animals, they constructed a large house in a tree, and they lived so happily on the island that when a ship came to rescue them, the parents and two of the sons decided not to leave.

Walt Disney's 1960 movie *Swiss Family Robinson* was
filmed on location in a giant mango tree on the
island of Tonga, but when I went to the Swiss Family
Robinson exhibit at Disney World I was appalled to
find a plastic treehouse in a reinforced-concrete tree.

*(overleaf)*
One of the pleasures of a treehouse is being able to
get away from the grownups.

These boys designed and built this substantial house themselves in an oak tree.

Children do not always take to treehouses built for them by grownups, but these young pirates look happy. This treehouse on Bainbridge Island, near Seattle, is perched on an enormous maple stump, and access to the house is through a staircase hollowed out of the center of the stump. The house is furnished with a bed and dartboard, and a large skylight brightens the interior.

Another treehouse built on a stump, this time a hollow elm near Guilford in Surrey, England.

Designed to resemble a lighthouse, it was constructed by a professional treehouse builder at a cost of $5,000.

Plastic-pipe playhouses constructed from kits may not fit everyone's image of a treehouse. However, they are sturdy, they go up quickly, and they can also be taken down quickly.

It doesn't take a beautiful tree to make a wonderful treehouse. This English treehouse is built on and around the trunks of several dead elms. Access is by a trap door in the floor.

This garden shed was built in a tree in London 15 years ago. It overlooks a school where former Prime Minister Margaret Thatcher used to hold meetings with her constituents, and the police eyed it with great suspicion.

This treehouse was built of old scaffolding planks and timber thrown out during the restoration of a ground house.

The "It's a Burl" woodworking shop in Cave Junction, Oregon, sells burlwood creations ranging from clocks to furniture. The owner of the shop even built this fanciful burlwood treehouse for his kids. A carved wizard holds up one corner of the platform. Plans call for a second platform and clubhouse above.

This daring treehouse was built in the late 1950s by students at Sherwood School in Ewell, Surrey, England. They used scrap lumber and other odds and ends and even equipped the house with a telephone. Ladders attached to the trunks and branches made the climb a little easier and safer. Many of the most imaginative and creative treehouses are built by children, and I feel that children's treehouses capture the essence of what a treehouse should be. Adults also build treehouses for kids, of course, but I often wonder who has more fun: the child who has a beautiful house built for him or the one who cobbles together his own house from scrap wood and rusty nails. I think I know the answer.

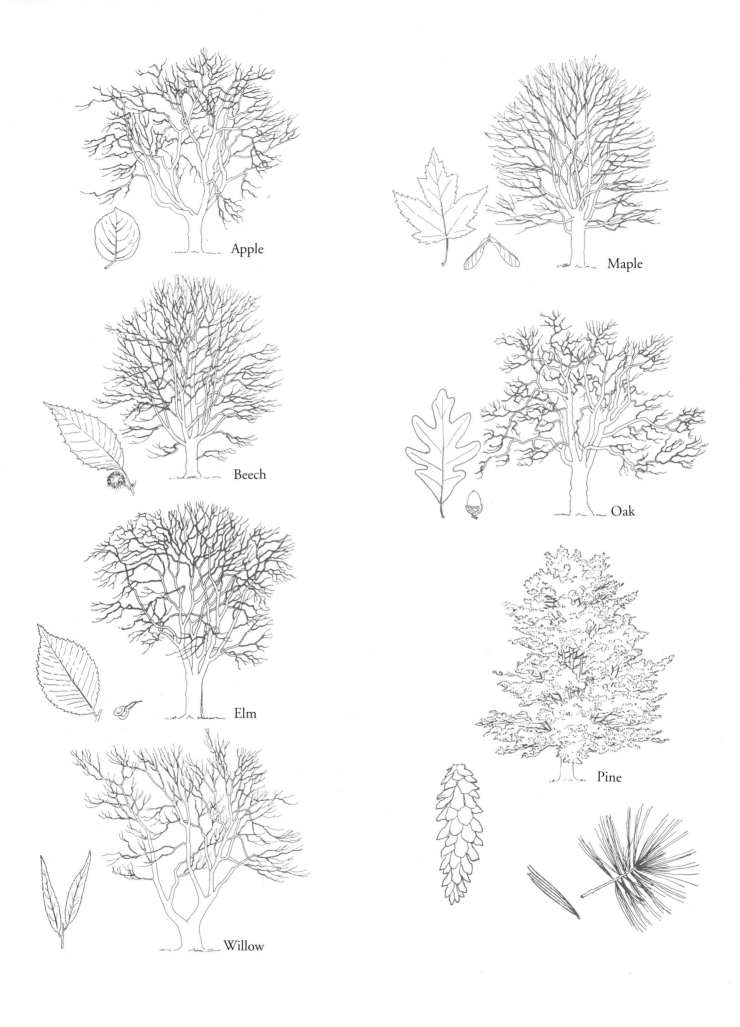

Apple

Maple

Beech

Oak

Elm

Pine

Willow

# FINDING THE RIGHT TREE

The right tree is determined partly by taste and partly by what kind of treehouse you want to build, but some trees are definitely wrong: trees that are too young, too old, too small, diseased, or rotted. Some species of trees are better than others — including maple, oak, fir, and hemlock—but whatever the species, any load-bearing branches should be at least six inches in diameter. For species with weaker wood, the branches should be larger, of course. Personally, I think the best tree to build in is one that opens up like a hand at a reasonable height above the ground ("reasonable" may mean eight feet or less for a kids' treehouse, with the sky the limit for adult treehouses). If you can't find a single tree that is just right, look for a cluster of trees suitable for a two-, three-, or four-tree house. Unless you have a sizable forest at hand, chances are you are not going to have a wide range of choices. In a typical suburban yard you will be lucky to find even one good site for a treehouse, so the problem is not so much to find the right tree as to figure out what kind of treehouse can be built in the tree that is available. If you want a big treehouse, you need a big tree. This enormous banyan is located outside of Hilo on the island of Hawaii. It was planted in 1902, and its owner claims it is the largest banyan in the United States.

# CONSTRUCTION

The basic construction methods used for treehouses are roughly the same as those used in houses built on the ground, but while most ground houses are more or less alike, every treehouse is different. The exact shape and structure of a treehouse are often dictated more by the tree than by the builder.

The first step in building any house is to create a level foundation. For a treehouse, this is usually done in one of three ways. The first is to lay beams across branches and shift them and shim them until they are level. The second is to run the beams between two or more tree trunks. The third is to cantilever the beams outward from a single trunk and support them with braces below or cables above. After the beams are leveled and secured to the tree, joists are laid across or between the beams, just as joists are laid across beams and foundation walls in building a house on the ground. The flooring is then nailed to the joists, and the platform is complete.

The platform must be attached securely to the tree, but not too securely. Trees bend, and a treehouse must bend with them. There are differences of opinion about how to attach the platform. Most treehouse builders use nails, spikes, screws, or lag bolts, but many refuse to drive even a single piece of metal into a tree. My feeling is that a few carefully driven nails or other fasteners do not do a tree any harm. What is harmful is anything that cuts the flow of nutrients through the cambium layer just below the bark. If the cambium layer is cut more than halfway around a branch or trunk, it can kill the branch or the whole tree. So if you suspend the treehouse from cables, be sure to wrap them in garden hose or use wooden blocking where they pass across the bark.

What goes on top of the platform depends on how fancy a treehouse you are building. The simplest treehouses have only a platform and a railing. Grander ones have walls, a roof, sometimes doors and windows — even fireplaces! From the platform up, treehouse construction is often just like ground house construction, except that lighter materials are frequently used, and allowances must be made for limbs passing through walls and other complications that rarely arise when building on the ground. For wall framing, I recommend the use of two-by-threes, which are lighter than two-by-fours but strong enough for most treehouses. I also recommend building the wall sections on the ground and then hoisting them onto the platform and nailing them down. Roofs can be built that way too. Just make sure that the sections don't get too heavy to lift.

By design, a treehouse can never be completely safe. However, a number of steps can be taken to avoid the most obvious dangers. One is to build a strong railing. Most building codes require a railing three feet high around any platform more than 18 inches off the ground, and the railing must have vertical balusters no more than six inches apart. Another safety feature, perhaps the most important, is not to build the treehouse too far off the ground in the first place, especially if it is intended for children. Eight feet should be exciting enough for most kids. Clear away any rocks or other protruding objects from around the base of the tree and cover the ground with bark mulch, sawdust, or sand. Of course, sturdy construction and easy access are essential to the safety of any treehouse.

# GETTING ALOFT

Access is a more critical question for a treehouse than a house on the ground. While there has to be some way of getting up the tree during construction, treehouse builders often improvise then and only build a permanent means of access after the house is completed. The most common means of access is a ladder, either wooden or rope. Rope ladders are simplest and have the advantage that you can pull the ladder up after you, making the treehouse very private. However, they can be hard to climb, as the bottom of the ladder swings away when you put your feet on it. This can be avoided by anchoring the ladder at the bottom as well as the top, but then of course you can't pull the ladder up. Wooden ladders can be freestanding or attached to the tree trunk, but do not simply nail lengths of board to the trunk and use them as treads. They can easily slip or pull loose.

Perhaps the safest means of access to a treehouse is a proper staircase, although some people may feel that stairs make a treehouse too much like a regular house. Building stairs requires careful measurements and carpentry. Any good book on homebuilding will show how to do it.

A fixed stairway leads to a fixed platform in this Oregon treehouse. Rather than letting the treehouse move with the trees, this builder employed the philosophy of letting the treehouse fix the trees in place. This can lead to trouble in high winds, but if the trees are as strong as these oaks, a fixed system can work well.

A hoist, such as a pulley or block and tackle, can be useful in constructing a treehouse and is almost essential if the house is built in sections on the ground. With a large enough hoist, an entire treehouse can be built on the ground and then lifted into the tree. Usually, the house is raised once and then secured to the tree and the hoist is removed, but some treehouse builders prefer a permanent hoist system.

Haig Markarian, of Tenafly, New Jersey, was 70 years old when he built his first treehouse. Wary of climbing the 80-foot oak in his backyard, he decided to build a treehouse that could be raised and lowered like an elevator. He constructed the house — six feet square with an eight-foot-high ceiling — in his garage, and furnished it with an easy chair, telephone, and radio. A tree surgeon anchored the hoist chain 60 feet up in the oak, and the chain ran down through the roof of the treehouse to an eight-horsepower electric hoist bolted to the floor. Operating the hoist with buttons and foot pedals,

Mr. Markarian would raise the treehouse 50 feet up, often at night so he could see the lights of the city. On one of his early voyages, the electric extension cord to the hoist pulled loose, and Mr. Markarian lost power with the treehouse near the top of its climb. He was stranded for hours until a neighbor rescued him by tossing the cord back up to Mr. Markarian. Since Mr. Markarian's death, his son Charles, shown in the photograph, has kept the treehouse in good working condition, but he doesn't like to take it more than 20 feet off the ground.

Strategically placed handles make a treehouse safer.

Strong railings are essential for a safe treehouse.

The lower platform of this treehouse is suspended from chains. When chains or cables are used to support a treehouse, they may be bolted to the branches or wrapped around them. If they are bolted, the bolts should run completely through the branches and be blocked on the back with large nuts and washers. When a chain or cable is wrapped around a branch, care must be taken to make sure the chain or cable doesn't cut into the branch. It should be wrapped in rubber hose or separated from the branch by wooden blocks. Branches will tend to bend over time when under constant strain, and it is important to make sure the branch is strong enough to support the weight of the treehouse. Don't attach a chain or cable too far out on a branch, and never attach one to a branch less than six inches in diameter.

A one-tree house built like a lean-to, with a blanket for a front door.

A two-tree house, supported by Y-shaped braces at each end.

Creativity and flexibility are the keys to treehouse construction. As this tree grows, the opening around the branch will have to be enlarged.

A three-tree house with a tentlike roof.          A four-tree house.

The following pages show, step by step, how to build sturdy one-tree and two-tree houses. Chances are, you won't want to build a house as substantial as these on your first try, but the basic techniques are applicable to any tree house. Because treehouses vary so much, I haven't included any specifications for lumber, nails, or other building materials. Any good carpenter or carpentry book should be able to help you decide what's right for your treehouse.

Building a One-Tree House

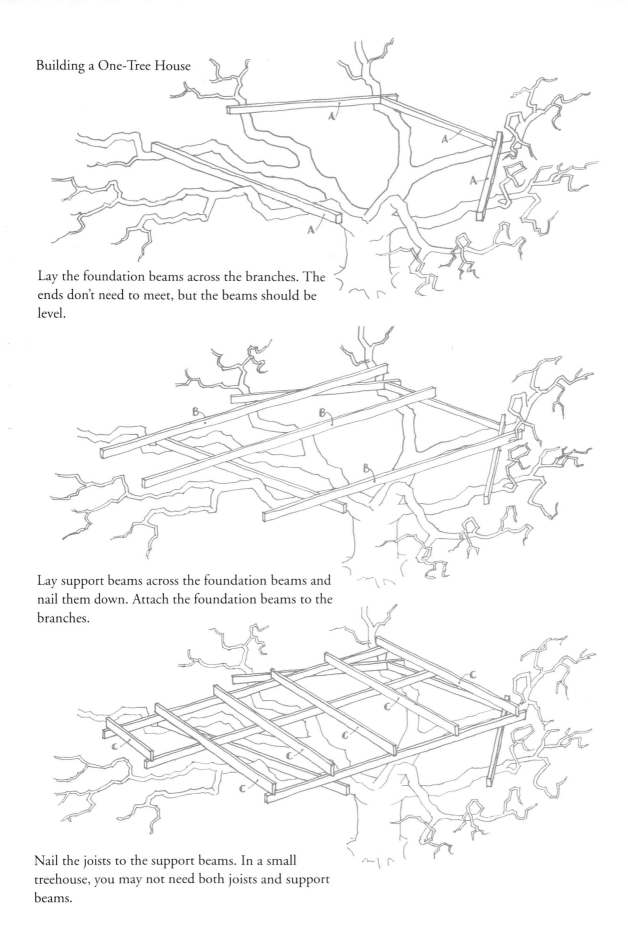

Lay the foundation beams across the branches. The ends don't need to meet, but the beams should be level.

Lay support beams across the foundation beams and nail them down. Attach the foundation beams to the branches.

Nail the joists to the support beams. In a small treehouse, you may not need both joists and support beams.

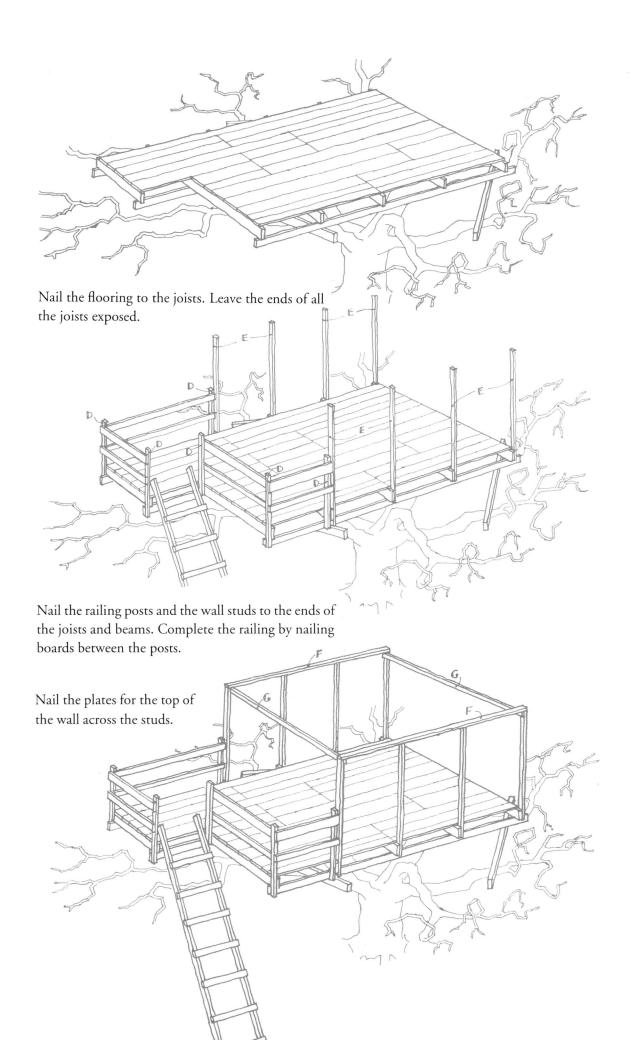

Nail the flooring to the joists. Leave the ends of all the joists exposed.

Nail the railing posts and the wall studs to the ends of the joists and beams. Complete the railing by nailing boards between the posts.

Nail the plates for the top of the wall across the studs.

Nail the supports for the ridgepole and the pole itself into place.

Nail the rafters to the wall plate and the ridgepole, then attach collar ties between the rafters. The ties keep the rafters and walls from spreading apart.

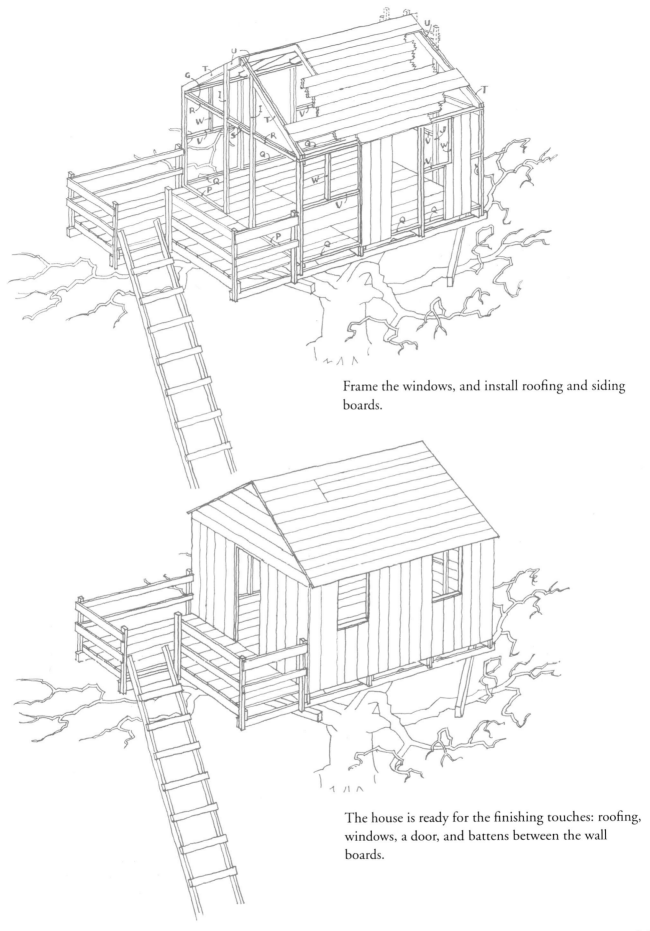

Frame the windows, and install roofing and siding boards.

The house is ready for the finishing touches: roofing, windows, a door, and battens between the wall boards.

Building a Two-Tree House

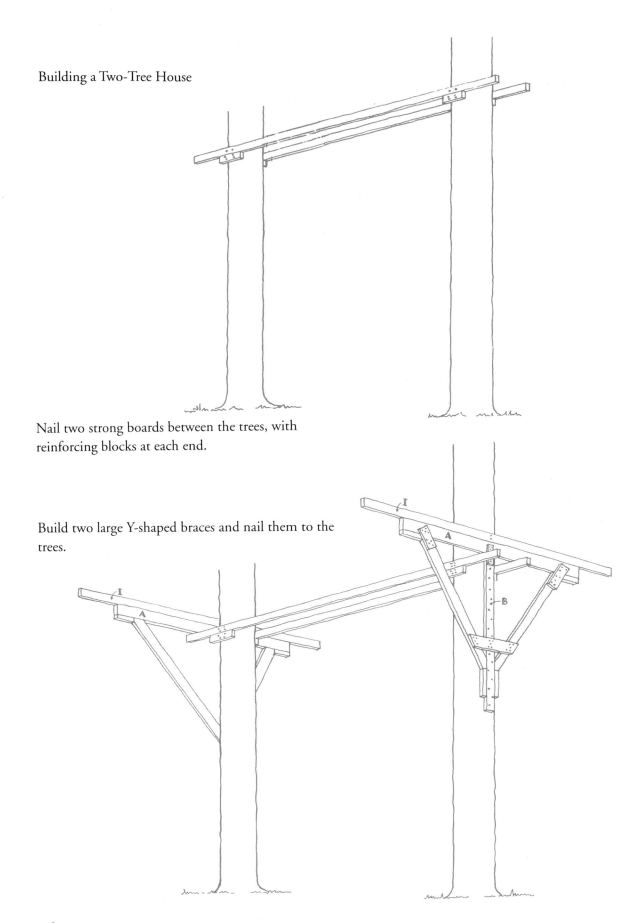

Nail two strong boards between the trees, with
reinforcing blocks at each end.

Build two large Y-shaped braces and nail them to the
trees.

Nail the joists to the braces.

Nail the flooring to the joists
and put up the railing.

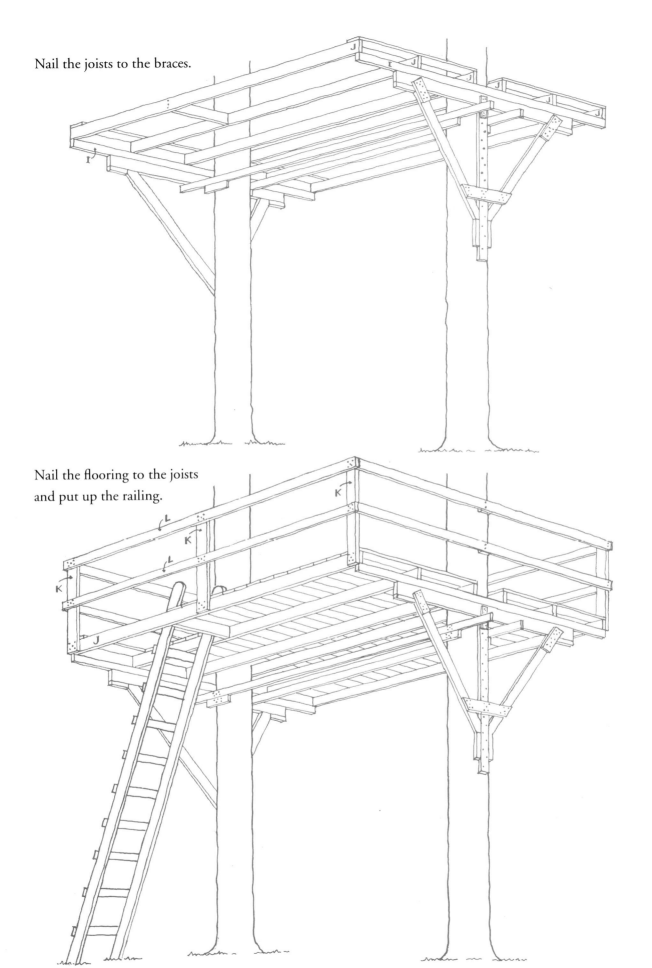

37

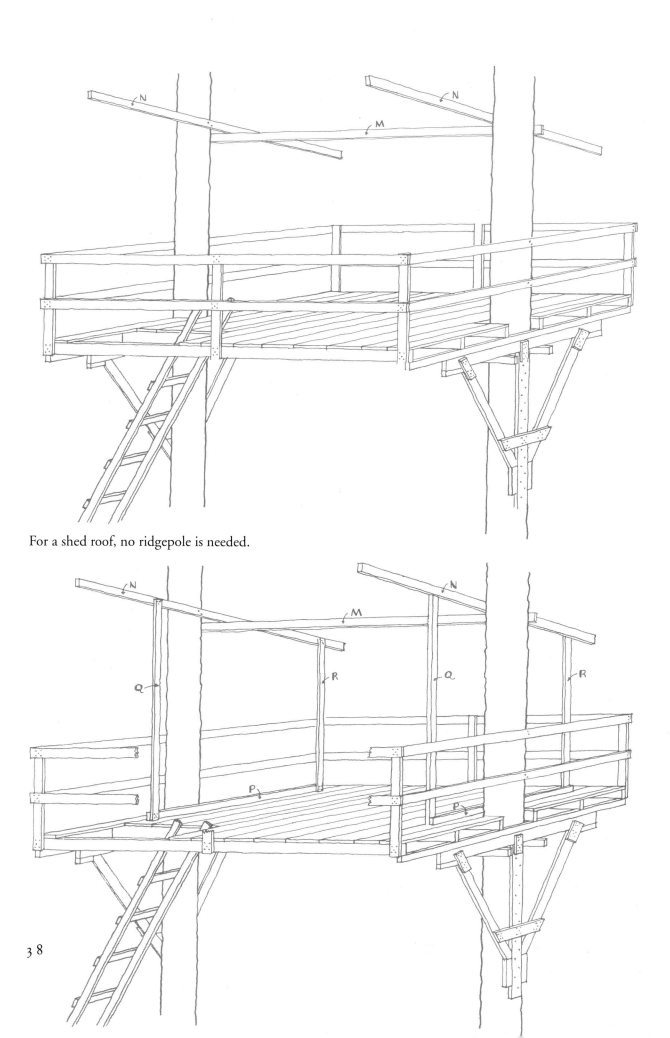

For a shed roof, no ridgepole is needed.

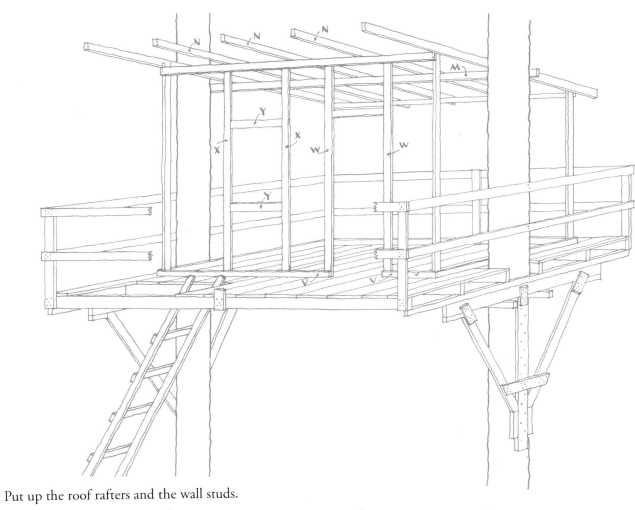

Put up the roof rafters and the wall studs.

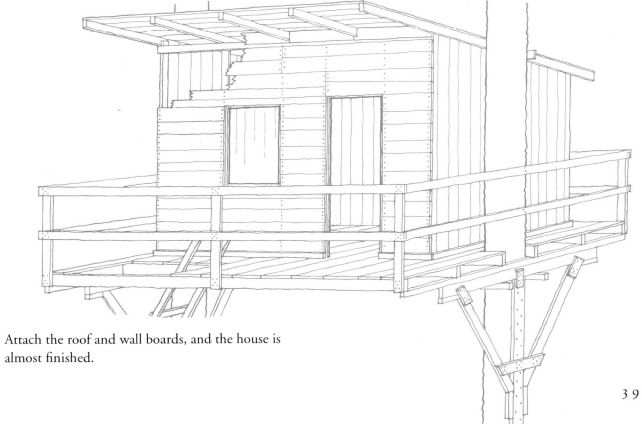

Attach the roof and wall boards, and the house is almost finished.

# THE SALTSPRING ISLAND TREEHOUSE

On an overcast February afternoon, my friend Charlie Kellogg and I drove north from Seattle toward Saltspring Island in British Columbia. Charlie's family owned some wooded land there on which I hoped to find the perfect treehouse tree. Hitting the ferries just right, we made it to the island by midnight and were up early the next morning, walking all over the 200 acres looking up at tree after tree after tree. But even with thousands of trees to choose from, it was hard to find one that was just right: this one was too small, that one leaned too much, this one had no view, and that one was too hard to get to.

By midafternoon our necks were sore, and we decided to take a break and go sea kayaking. We soon found ourselves in the midst of a pod of orca whales, and when a large male orca almost capsized my kayak, we paddled quickly back to shore. Then, hiking up the path behind Charlie's cabin, I suddenly found myself staring at the tree of my dreams.

It was a huge fir tree, maybe 150 feet high and nearly six feet in diameter at the base, and it stood majestically at the base of a 30-foot moss-covered rock outcropping in a small grove of other giant firs. Its many branches had probably saved it from the saw when the property was selectively logged a century ago, but they made it ideal for a treehouse. The only flaw I could see was a slight lean, but I figured we could easily correct for that during construction. That evening I sketched the preliminary plans. The next day we took careful measurements of the tree and headed back to Seattle.

A stretch of British Columbia's idyllic coastal waters separates Saltspring Island from Vancouver Island. This photo was taken on Saltspring.

Along the shady gullies that are etched in Saltspring's mountainous west slope grow temperate rain forests with a wide variety of lush vegetation. The land was selectively logged more than a century ago, but many large fir trees were left behind, and some of them have now grown to as much as 10 feet in diameter.

The west elevation. This side of the treehouse looks
out on the water and the mountains of Vancouver
Island in the distance, and on Charlie's cabin and a
field in the foreground.

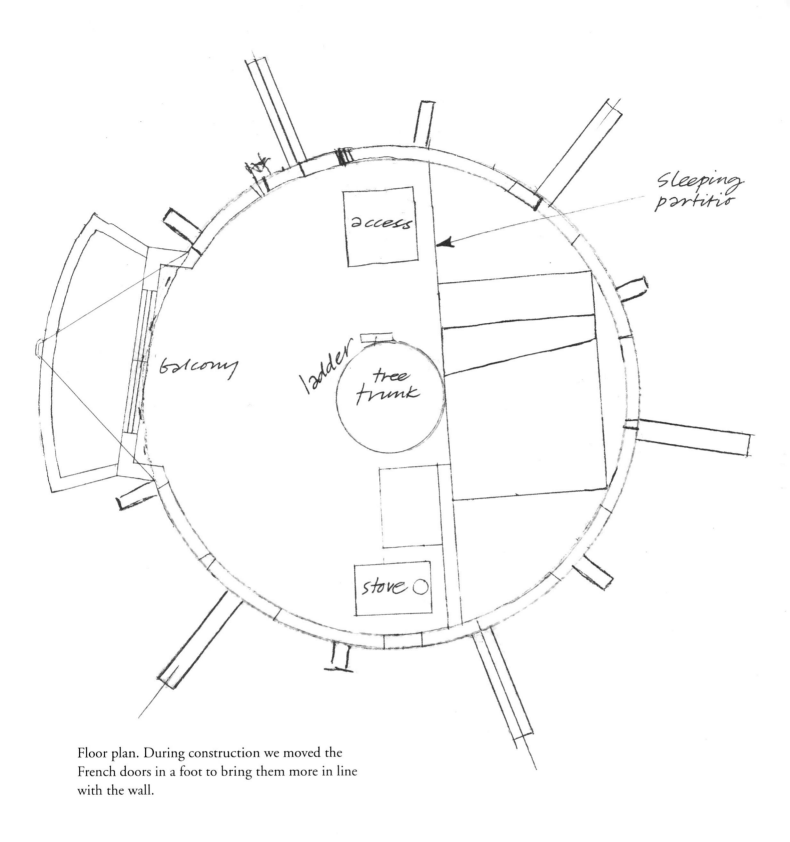

Floor plan. During construction we moved the French doors in a foot to bring them more in line with the wall.

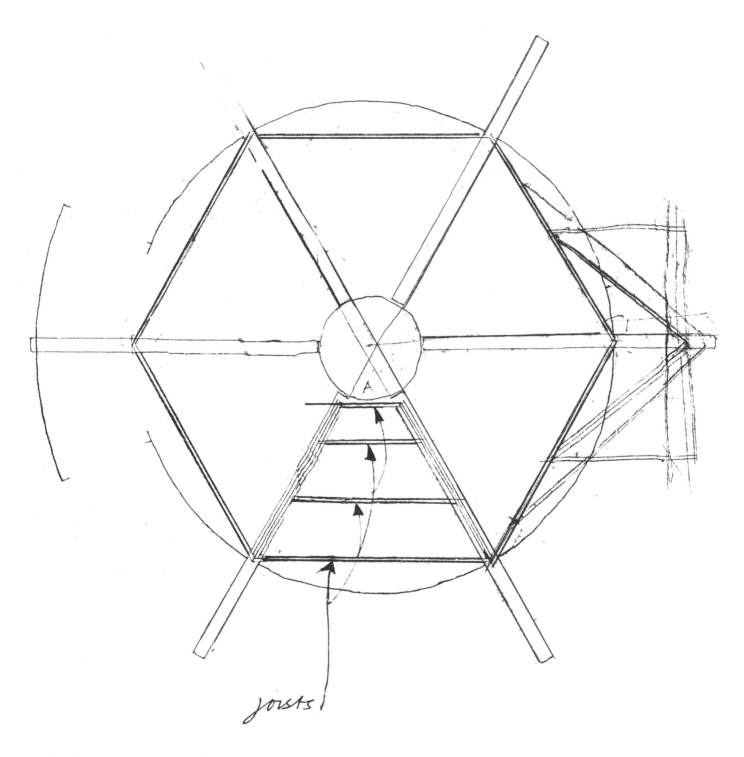

*joists!*

The floor joist layout. When we found rot in the
two-by-sixes we were going to use as floor joists, we
had to redesign the layout slightly. The end result
used less wood and was just as strong.

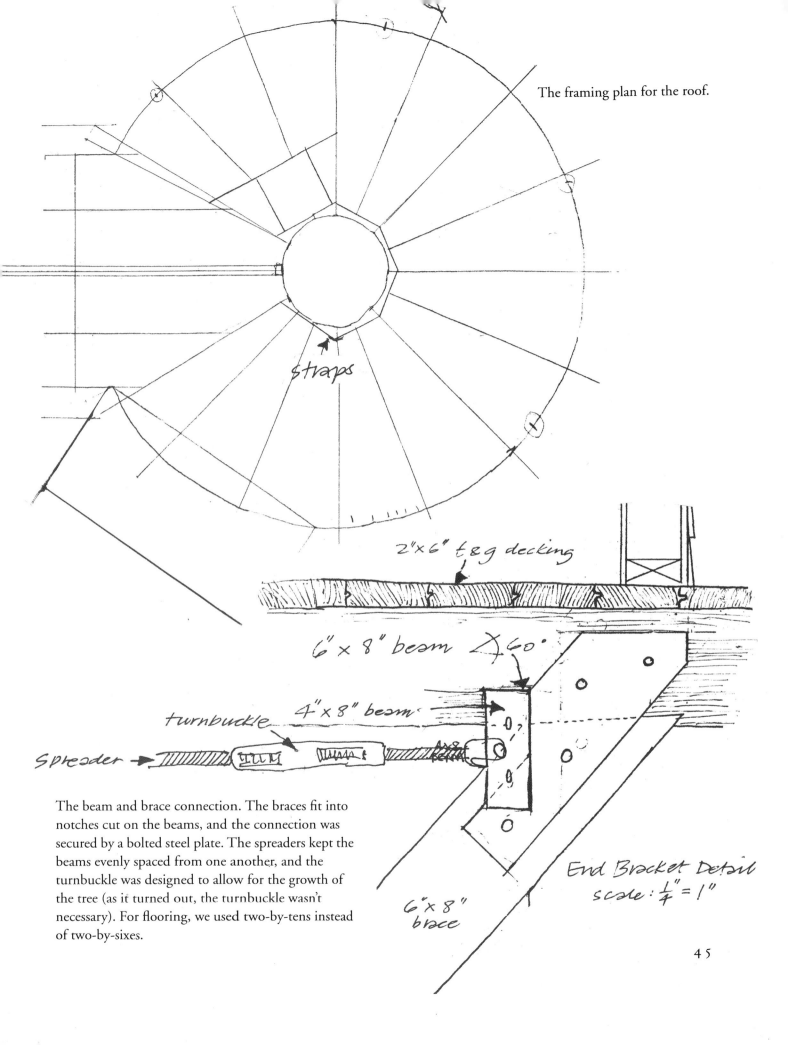

The framing plan for the roof.

straps

2"x6" t&g decking

6"x8" beam ⟩ 60°

4"x8" beam

turnbuckle

Spreader →

End Bracket Detail
scale: $\frac{1}{4}$" = 1"

6"x8" brace

The beam and brace connection. The braces fit into notches cut on the beams, and the connection was secured by a bolted steel plate. The spreaders kept the beams evenly spaced from one another, and the turnbuckle was designed to allow for the growth of the tree (as it turned out, the turnbuckle wasn't necessary). For flooring, we used two-by-tens instead of two-by-sixes.

45

Five months later we returned to the island in a truck loaded with lumber, tar paper, roof shingles, wall shingles, roofing tar, windows and window casings, doors, hinges, flashing; lag bolts, carriage bolts, screws, staples, and nails of every size; table saw, chain saw, chop saw, circular saw, hand saws; nail guns, staple guns, drills, bits, and augers; ladders, extension cords, pulleys, and rope—miles and miles of rope. Bright and early on a beautiful July morning, we started building. I hoped to have the house finished in a week.

Day 1. The first order of business was to empty and organize the truckload of building materials and tools we had driven up from Seattle. I had hoped that we would have time to erect a few beams and braces, but the unloading took so long we were only able to set our safety lines and mark the treehouse's floor level on the trunk of the fir.

Day 2. The first hole we drilled in the tree hit sawdust at a depth of six inches. I remembered the stories loggers had told me about rotten trees snapping in two, or "telescoping," killing everyone below. However, our second hole found solid wood to a depth of 14 inches, and we never struck sawdust again. By the end of the day we had the first beam and brace pair bolted into position on the tree. The following day we would discover that I had set the brace bracket precisely one foot too high on the

trunk of the tree. Thereafter I was relegated to supervising construction of the platform from below. We cut the beams and braces on the ground and then hoisted them into the tree. They were made from massive six-by-eights so thick that the circular saw couldn't cut through them even in two passes. We had to finish the job with a handsaw. Each beam and brace was bolted to the tree trunk with a metal bracket.

The six-by-eights were green and heavy, some of them weighing over 250 pounds. We hoisted them with a heavy-duty boat pulley and 1/2-inch nylon rope. A block and tackle would have made the job easier.

Day 3. Because the tree leaned slightly, each brace had to be cut to a different length in order to keep the floor level. First, we would hoist a beam into position and pin it into its bracket on the trunk. Then crew members standing on the ground would pull on the hoisting ropes to level the beam. With the beam level, we would measure the length of brace needed. The brace would be cut on the ground, hoisted up, and fitted into the beam. We worked our way around the

tree, with each beam and brace pair taking over an hour to complete. This system worked almost perfectly, except for the brace bracket I set a foot too high on the trunk. Rather than move the bracket we decided to cut a shorter brace and hope no one would notice. All six pairs were in place by the end of the day, but I was beginning to doubt that we could finish the house in seven days.

The final brace is hoisted up, with the side plates already loosely in place.

I spent much of the first few days on the ground looking up, watching, worrying, waiting for Charlie to climb down from the tree with the latest bad news. However insoluble a problem might seem, we always found a solution.

The lines hang down like multicolored vines. The line and harness system worked well, allowing us to dance around the tree in safety and comfort (after we lost·all feeling in our legs) as we attached brackets, beams, and braces.

Day 4. We awoke to a driving rain on Tuesday, but that didn't stop several new people from joining the crew, including Charlie's older brother Gaylord, who showed up sporting a brand-new tool belt full of shiny new tools. I put him in charge of quality control. Charlie explained our work rules to the newcomers: no radios, no climbing without a secured harness, and no consumption of alcohol except by the hoistmaster, who was allowed reasonable amounts of beer. In seven hours of hard, wet work we installed all the remaining bolts, stabilized the beams with spreaders, and cut the plywood for the exterior walls. Most of us were in bed by nine that night.

Even after they were bolted to the trunk of the tree, the beams and braces still had a fair amount of side-to-side play. We had to install spreaders to fix them an equal distance from each other. First we nailed in temporary wooden spreaders, then we installed permanent spreaders cut from steel rod. Here John Rouches (left) maneuvers the beam and checks the tape measure, while Charlie Kellogg (right) waits to nail the spreader down. Kipp Stroden (background) was installing bolts.

John and Charlie install the permanent spreaders, made of 3/4-inch threaded rod with a turnbuckle. I figured that as the tree trunk grew, it would push the beams outward, so I included a turnbuckle in each spreader to allow for expansion. However, Charlie pointed out that the brackets holding the beams and braces were lag-bolted into the heartwood of the tree, which was no longer growing. As the tree grew, it would simply grow around the brackets, rather than pushing the beams outward. Simple wood spreaders without turnbuckles would have worked just fine.

Kipp keeps on bolting, while Charlie grabs a bucket of turnbuckles hoisted from below.

John Rouches drills bolt holes and lag-bolts the braces to the brackets attached to the trunk.

Since the wall curved, the horizontal pieces—the top plate and the bottom sill—had to curve too, so we made them from two layers cut from $3/4$-inch plywood instead of two-by-fours. Here we are constructing the sill. First, the curved pieces were hoisted up and laid down, with joints staggered, in a double ring. Then we temporarily nailed the ring onto the beams so we could mark the location of the wall sections. Finally, the ring was cut into six sections, which were lowered to the ground so that the six wall sections could be framed on top of them.

The view from below with the sill plates nailed down temporarily.

John Rouches adjusts the knot on his safety line while sitting on one of the massive beams. The knot is made from a strong loop of ¹/₂-inch nylon rope that wraps three times around the main safety line and then back through a carabiner on John's harness. The loop can be slipped easily up and down the line, but will cinch up tightly with any sudden pull.

Day 5. The rain had subsided, but the day got off to a gloomy start. The two-by-six floor joists were to be assembled on the ground into six triangular sections that would fit together like the slices of a pie. The sections would then be hoisted up and nailed into place on top of the beams. But after we had raised the first section, Charlie climbed down from the tree and solemnly informed me that the two-by-sixes were showing signs of rot. When a careful examination showed that all the joists were rotted, I took out my frustration by pounding them with my framing hammer. It made me feel a lot better, and fortunately, Charlie, as usual, had a solution: We could take the two-by-sixes we had marked for the roof rafters and use them for the floor. Someone could drive to town and bring back new two-by-sixes by the time we would need them for the roof. Since there were not enough roof rafters to build the floor joist sections as designed, we had to change the plans, eliminating one joist per section and nailing the joists directly in place rather than prefabricating the sections on the ground. The work took longer, but the structure was just as strong and used less lumber.

In the end, it was a very productive day, for we not only completed all the joists but assembled the first wall section on the ground. There was one terrifying moment, however. Charlie and Kipp were up in the tree, and I was out in the field, when I heard an awful thud, as if something large had hit the ground. My view was blocked by brush, and when I heard Charlie say, "Don't move!" my heart stopped. "Kipp?" I yelled, and rushed to the tree, expecting to find him lying on the ground. But all I found was his hammer, which he asked me to hoist back up to him. Kipp had stepped on the wrong end of a board resting between beams and fallen one frightening foot before being caught by his harness. It seems Charlie and I were more shaken than Kipp was. I spent the next several minutes walking around reminding everyone of the safety rules.

The substructure is complete, with the two-by-six floor joists riding on top of the beams.

Day 6. Thursday, we nailed the floor to the joists, finished building the wall sections on the ground, and even hoisted the first wall section into position. Late that night, the fourth John of the crew, John "Cougar" Tyler, arrived with the new roof rafters and the rest of the materials needed to finish the job—or so I thought at the time.

The braces and beams were fastened together securely with steel plates. The plates were bolted to the braces on the ground, using 3/4-inch carriage bolts that ran completely through the brace from one plate to the other. We used lag bolts to attach the plates to the beams, however. The through-bolts required precise holes that would have been difficult to drill while dangling from a rope 30 feet in the air.

With the substructure complete, we began to lay out the floor.

We used two-by-tens for the floor, mainly because I had a lot of two-by-tens left over from another job. The boards were laid out in a sunburst pattern, radiating from the trunk of the tree. This required precise cutting with the circular saw and jigsaw, but it resulted in a very handsome floor.

The last floorboard is hoisted onto the platform.

In midafternoon of the sixth day, we finished laying the floor and paused for a photograph. Left to right, seated, are John Rouches and Charlie Kellogg, and standing, Kipp Stroden, Michael Robb, John MacKenzie, and Gaylord Kellogg. I'm kneeling in the middle.

Charlie and I go over new plans for the entry hatch in the floor of the house, while in the background John MacKenzie and Gaylord frame a wall section.

The wall was composed of six curved sections. We built the sections on the ground and then hoisted them up into the treehouse. This worked so well it led me to formulate a general rule of treehouse construction: build as much as possible on the ground; it's safer and easier. Just be sure that what you build is light enough to be lifted. Even our heaviest wall sections weighed less than some of the beams. In this case, size was more of a concern than weight, because we had to lift the wall sections through the lower branches of the tree.

The wall sections were fairly standard construction, with two-by-four studs and $1/2$-inch plywood sheathing. However, the curve of the wall necessitated a couple of changes: the top plate and sill plate were each made of two layers of $3/4$-inch plywood, rather than two-by-fours, and the sheathing had to be grooved, or kerfed, from top to bottom to allow it to bend. We kerfed it $3/16$ of an inch deep every six inches or so.

Framing the windows and doors was tricky. Here John MacKenzie and I are installing the crippler that holds up the header over a window.

The walls had to be laid out carefully so that the windows and doors would all end up in their proper locations. The spacing of the windows on either side of the French doors was most crucial.

On goes the plywood sheathing. We extended the sheathing eight inches below the sill plate so that it would cover the ends of the floor joists.

Oops. The first wall section got caught on a branch as it was going up. It was finally freed with much tugging and shouting, and Gaylord, the hoistmaster, was sent back to the drawing board to devise a better system, which he did by moving the hoist and the ropes.

We finally got the first section up.

64

Temporary scaffolding was nailed to the ends of the beams so we would have a place to stand while doing the exterior work.

Day 7. Friday was a busy day: We hoisted the remaining wall sections into position, hung all the roof rafters, and installed the windows and door jamb. By evening the end of the job was in sight, and we all relaxed on the front porch of Charlie's cabin, looking out over the trees and water to the mountains of Vancouver Island in the distance. The sun didn't set until 9:30, and few of us stayed up late enough to see the stars come out.

The wall sections went up quickly, fitting neatly into one another. We had to hoist the fourth wall section in an unfinished state because of the large branch that would have to poke through it. The opening to the left of the branch was supposed to be a small window, but we decided to eliminate it and move the opening over to accomodate the branch.

Of course, we couldn't put glass in the opening with the branch passing through it, but eventually I plan to install a flexible neoprene collar to make it more weathertight.

When the the final wall section had been placed in position, we began installing the headers over the windows. The large gap in the wall is where the French doors will go.

We installed most of the wall sheathing on the ground, except for the ends that would curve around and bridge the gaps between the wall sections. Once the sections were hoisted into the tree and nailed in place we nailed down the free edges and filled the remaining spaces where needed. We had to widen some of the rough window openings, too. Getting the walls ready for the roof and windows took nearly half a day.

After all the wall sections were in position, we nailed a second layer of $^3/_4$-inch plywood around the top, connecting the sections more securely and providing a strong base for the rafters to rest on.

Kipp applies some finishing touches to the sheathing.

*(left)* The house was beginning to look like a water tower with a few odd holes.

To support the rafters, we constructed a collar around the trunk of the tree, building it up from three layers of $1/2$-inch plywood. The rafters were nailed to the collar rather than directly to the tree.

Charlie and John MacKenzie mark the cuts for the roof rafters.

Day 8: The eighth day of construction was a Saturday and brought an influx of new volunteers. The treehouse was now at a stage where three or more crews could be working at once, and the progress was astounding. One crew covered the interior wall in tongue-and-groove cedar, while another shingled the exterior, and a third sheathed the roof. We had our usual crises, of course. Charlie, running the roofing crew, discovered that the pie-shaped pieces of $5/8$-inch plywood we had cut for the roof sheathing were too short. We had to add a short section of $1/2$-inch plywood to create the desired 10-inch overhang.

John Tyler takes a break from shingling to admire Kipp's work on the interior. Charlie Kellogg and John MacKenzie nail down the roofing under Gaylord Kellogg's supervision.

Day 9: Sunday was the last full day of construction, and many of the crew had to catch a late afternoon ferry back to the city. We were in the home stretch, but there were many big jobs remaining: hanging the doors, building the door and window casings, and completing the shingling and roofing.

John MacKenzie and Charlie spent another day on the roof.

It turned out I hadn't brought enough roofing material, but Charlie's neighbor Chris saved the day when he arrived on Sunday with some asphalt shingles left over from a house he was building. The new shingles were lighter in color, so the roof looks a little strange. But then, few people are going to see it from this angle. I wanted the house to look as natural as it is possible for a house to look 30 feet up in a tree, and I was pleased with the way it was turning out. This is the south side of the house.

The French doors were made by a German craftsman I met when he was housesitting for my next-door neighbors. A contractor had commissioned him to build the doors for a large lakefront house on Mercer Island near Seattle. He spent countless hours designing and building the doors, but through some miscommunication they ended up two inches short. The contractor wouldn't accept them, so I was able to buy them at a steep discount. Each panel is made up of 143 pieces of cut glass joined by zinc strips. When the sun shines through the doors, the glass refracts the light, spraying a spectrum of colors around the interior of the treehouse.

The Straits of Georgia and Vancouver Island can be glimpsed through the French doors.

The curve of the bargeboard above the doors matches the curve of the treehouse walls. Charlie plans to design and carve a Northwest Indian motif on the barge.

Day 10. Monday we installed the baseboard and crown trim and cleaned up the construction site. The very last thing we did was hoist up the furniture, but we didn't have time to sit and relax because we had to rush to make the ferry.

The house is 16 feet across and has nearly 200 square
feet of floor space. With the sunlight pouring
through the windows and doors it feels even larger.
Fifty people could easily fit inside, and the structure is
strong enough to support them. The rope around the
tree trunk is a safety line we can use when climbing
the ladder.

I had estimated the treehouse would take five or six people about a week to complete, but to my surprise, 22 friends came to lend a hand. The project took 10 days and over 500 man-hours. It was worth it, though, and I will be eternally grateful to all those who helped, especially the hard core of Charlie Kellogg, John Rouches, John MacKenzie, Gaylord Kellogg, Mike Robb, Kipp Stroden, and John Tyler.

The interior walls were clad in six-inch tongue-and-groove cedar that two people were able to install in a few hours. The window casings were a little more work, since the horizontal pieces had to be kerfed to follow the curve of the walls. At first the doors opened onto a 33-foot drop, but later we built a deck with pressure-treated two-by-six joists.

When Mark Tucker of St. Louis Park, Minnesota, set out to build a treehouse for his son, he expected the job to take three days. It has now consumed six years of his life, landed him in jail, and broken up his marriage. Once Mark started building, he couldn't stop, and eventually the town building department stepped in and ordered him to tear down the house or bring it up to code. The media picked up the story, which led to the discovery that a few rental properties he owned needed some improvements too. His tenants filed suit and won a $100,000 judgment. When Mark couldn't pay, he was locked up briefly, whereupon his wife left him and filed for divorce. Their home ended up in the hands of a bank, but Mark was able to buy it back and continue work on the treehouse, this time in cooperation with the town engineers. He has now spent an estimated 3,000 hours on the treehouse and still is not finished. One of the latest additions is a special platform near the crow's nest where he hopes to be remarried to his former wife some day.

Mark, an insurance broker, has an office in the treehouse, which also contains a guest room.

The builder of this treehouse was formerly known as Freedom Arrow, leader of the Clearlight hippie tribe in Seattle, Washington. After years of guiding his flock, he retired to the Northern California coast. One morning as he was drinking coffee in a shorefront restaurant in Point Arena, he prophesied that a storm or tidal wave was about to strike the area. After a wave did strike, destroying the restaurant, he changed his name to Ocean Oracle, and the stunned owners let Oracle salvage as much lumber as he needed for the treehouse he was building. (In return, they asked him not to issue any more prophecies about Point Arena.) One of the finer touches in Oracle's remarkably uninhibited design is the use of his VW van's windshield as one of the large windows on the east side of the treehouse.

Grog, a 43-year-old skydiver with over 1,750 jumps to his credit, talked for years about building a treehouse. When a crash landing put his plane out of commission seven years ago, he finally got down to work. First he leaned an old staircase against the tree; he climbed the staircase and then continued on to the top of the tree, where he installed a pulley to use in hoisting materials. Climbing back down to the top of the stairs, he built a platform there, set up a ladder on that platform, climbed the ladder to build another platform, and so forth until he was 60 feet off the ground. There he built his house. The day I visited, Grog was off skydiving, and he told me later that his chute had opened at a bad angle and sent him careening into his jumping partner. Grog managed to cut loose his main chute and open his backup at 800 feet, but his partner didn't get his open until 200 feet and broke 12 bones when he landed. After the jump, Grog learned that his first grandson had been born as he was going down, and he joked that they were both probably screaming at the same time. "Out with the old, in with the new," he said philosophically. When the wind blows, being in Grog's house is like being in a boat at sea. Even Grog says, "A gentle breeze is one thing, but when it's howling this is no place to be."

The ladders are sturdily built, and the platforms and handrails make the climb easier. Still, I felt a little queasy as I made my way up the highest ladder. The walls, like the ladders, were constructed on the ground and hoisted up by pulley.

Once aloft, queasiness gives way to wonder, at least when the wind isn't blowing. Since the tree is on a steep hillside, the view of the Applegate Valley below is even more spectacular. It's like being in a hot air balloon.

Gary and Linda Norris built their island vacation house 30 feet up in a western red alder with four trunks 18 to 24 inches in diameter. It took them a week of 10-hour days to construct the platform and shell and three more years to finish the interior and scrounge the furnishings. All of the work was done by hand, with no power tools. The house is seven feet wide and 10 feet long, with a four-foot deck. It has hardwood floors, pine ceilings, leaded glass and crystal front doors, a convertible sofa, gas lamps, and a small woodburning stove for heating and cooking. The most impressive furnishing, though, is the spectacular waterfront view of Whidbey Island and the Olympic Mountains.

The Norris treehouse was the first I saw that used a floating foundation system. Four large metal brackets are bolted to the four trunks, and the two main beams float freely between the brackets. Thus, as the trees bend with the breeze, the treehouse can move with them. To keep the beams from wandering off their brackets in a high wind, Gary, a fireman from Seattle, threaded a piece of fire hose through the back of each bracket and nailed it to the beam.

"It was a real joy to come home and build the treehouse after a hectic day at work," Gary told me. "I think that one of the really neat things about a treehouse is that you know it is not always going to be there. You know that any day it could be blown down. So when you are there you appreciate it more."

This classic Victorian treehouse in downtown Seattle was built between 1890 and 1910. It is now surrounded by large apartment buildings and Interstate 5, but its view of the Olympic Mountains has not been blocked. The five-foot-diameter fir stump that serves as its foundation is a startling reminder of the old-growth forest that once grew where Seattle now sprawls. A cedar or redwood stump would last better, but this stump has held up reasonably well for a fir. However, it has had numerous repairs over the years, including metal straps that were wrapped around its perimeter some time back. Twenty years ago, posts of four-by-four cedar were added at the corners of the treehouse when it was discovered that the main supports over the stump were rotted. The rampant wisteria blooms in beautiful purple bunches in the spring. Judging from the thickness of the wisteria vine, it was probably planted by the original owner of the treehouse, who had the house built for his grandchildren. Now one of his great-grandchildren owns it and hopes one day to have it restored.

*(opposite)* In a neighborhood of ranch houses, cottages, and trailers in Eureka, California, it is astonishing to look up and see two small houses perched on redwoods, looking as if they had sprouted naturally from the treetops. They were built by a crabber named Earl Harvey as a sort of memorial to his son, who drowned when their boat was wrecked on a rocky shore in 1971. After his son's death, Harvey began collecting driftwood and limbs from lumbered redwoods and spent four years building these treehouses, which became a great attraction for the children of the neighborhood. He even created an unusual kind of wishing well in one of the houses, wrapping a one-inch hose around the trunk of the tree from the house to the ground. Children would make a wish, drop a coin in a slot at the top, and listen to the coin rattling down the hose to the collection box at the bottom. The other house had a wood stove. Mr. Harvey moved four years ago but the new owners, Donna McMartin and Kevin Smith, have continued the tradition of letting children play in the houses. In these litigious days, however, they must be closely supervised.

Each treehouse sits on top of a "double split" (forked) redwood, and both trees are still very much alive. Kevin has to prune a path up the winding stairways every year, although one year the pruning was done by a hungry goat. Earl Harvey supported the staircases with steel rebar, or concrete reinforcement bars, that he drove into the trunks of the trees. The houses have weathered well, and the rebar does not seem to have hurt the trees.

To reach the isolated hermitage built by a group of Franciscan monks, I followed a back road through the Berkshires of western Massachusetts until I found what looked like an overgrown tractor path leading deeper into the woods. The trail dropped down through the forest for a half mile to a beaver dam and a marsh with a very rickety wooden bridge leading across it. Under the watchful gaze of one of the beavers, I drove very slowly and carefully across the bridge and came out in a field, where I parked the car. A footpath led into a mature forest of maples, birches, white pine, and hemlock, and as I walked along the flower-lined path, listening to the babbling of the beavers' brook, the magic of the hermitage began to envelop me. I crossed another bridge leading over the brook where it broadened into a small pond, and looking up the hill to my right I saw a large boulder with a tiny chapel on top of it. Farther up the hill beyond the chapel was the hermitage's treehouse. Only one monk, Brother Michael, is left of the group that built the hermitage. He visits the treehouse only occasionally, but others often use it as a spiritual retreat.

*(above)* These twin treehouses seem to float on a forest of billowing hachu tree ferns on the slopes of Mount Hualalai. They were built on Allen Beall's 60-acre estate by Beall's caretaker, Curtis Keonelehua Yim Cook, Curtis's friend Pancho Pitler, and Beall's son Corry. Only Pancho had any carpentry experience, and the work took four months using standard framing techniques. They anchored each house to the trunk of a tall Ohea tree and supported the corners with 20- to 25-foot posts resting on the ground. To allow for the movement of the tree, they left a 10-inch gap between the roof and the trunk. The gap is covered by an expandable cone-shaped piece of flashing that is attached to the trunk and overhangs the roof opening by six inches. The houses are built in typical Hawaiian cottage style with wraparound decks, and they are the best furnished treehouses I have seen, with iron clawfoot bathtubs, high-tank toilets, hot and cold running water, centrally plumbed gas lanterns, and queen-sized bunk beds. Each had a stove and refrigerator until the building department ordered them removed for fear that someone might move into the houses permanently.

*(left)* Like the treehouse, the chapel can comfortably accomodate only one person at a time. The treehouse has a beautiful view of the pond and the surrounding forest.

While visiting his parents in central Florida, Kendall Thurston, a 35-year-old cabinetmaker from upstate New York, decided that the giant live oaks growing there were just begging for a treehouse. So he built one, 40 feet up in a tree on the banks of the Suwannee River. First, using a come-along and a block and tackle, he hoisted up two 20-foot-long 350-pound telephone poles and four 20-foot beams and laid the beams across the poles to form the foundation for the house. The poles rested on the tree at three points and were supported at a fourth point by a heavy chain attached to a main branch above. Two-by-six joists were then nailed to the beams, and two-by-six decking was laid across the joists to complete the platform. As is often the case in treehouse construction, the 20-by-20-foot platform was not perfectly square. Following the shape of the tree, it came out as a parallelogram with corners of 75 and 105 degrees.

The view from the sleeping loft, looking down on the kitchen area. Water for cooking and washing came from a neighbor's tap and had to be hoisted up from below. The stove on the counter and the refrigerator below it are fueled by propane.

(opposite) During a late spring flood, Kendall climbs the rope ladder to his treehouse 40 feet above the Suwannee River. In the dry summer months, the river is often far below the banks. Kendall anchored his ladder at the bottom to keep it from swinging as he climbed.

A wood stove warms the house on winter nights, which can be surprisingly cool along the Suwannee, and the roof is insulated with one inch of rigid foam. The insulation not only holds in the heat but softens the drumming of the rain on the metal roof. To save weight, particularly since the wall and roof sections were built on the ground and hoisted up, the house walls were framed with one-by-threes and the roof with two-by-threes. Diagonal bracing strengthened the wall and roof sections. Kendall encourages visitors to write on the walls.

Where the platform rested on tree limbs, it floated freely to keep the house from being torn apart when the tree bent in high winds. When the platform was finished, Kendall built the house in sections on the ground and lifted them into position in the tree. The sheathing, siding, and roofing were applied after the sections were hoisted into the tree and nailed down. The walls were covered with $1/2$-inch plywood sheathing and bevel siding. For the roof, lightweight 16-gauge aluminum roofing was attached directly to the rafters. The weight of the house, an estimated 4,300 pounds, helped to stabilize it in the tree. Kendall built the house single-handedly in six months and lived there for four years. Unfortunately, his lease on the tree was an oral one, and when the farmer who owned the land sold it to a developer, he was evicted. He tried to buy the lot where the tree grew, but apparently treehouses did not fit the developer's plans and Kendall's offer was rejected.

When Kendall was evicted from the tree by a new landowner, he found a friend of a friend who knew a helicopter pilot who agreed to fly the house to a new site. Here Kendall makes the lines ready as the chopper hovers overhead.

An unlikely sight: a helicopter hauling a treehouse down the Suwanee at 50 miles an hour. Kendall followed along in his boat.

Kendall and friends wave goodbye to the pilot after the house was safely landed in a cotton field three miles from its former site.

The rate card for this one-room hotel in Hawaii carries a note from the proprietor, Linda Beech: "Occasionally, a few days each year (about ten), Waipi'o Tree House is inaccessible because of high river water. Should guests be unable to leave, food and lodging during their delay are complimentary." The house rests 25 feet up in a giant monkeypod tree overlooking the Waipi'o Valley, site of one of the first settlements in the Hawaiian Islands. The Polynesian settlers brought with them seeds of plants from throughout the Pacific rim, including the monkeypod, a native of South America. If there was ever a tree meant for a treehouse, it's the monkeypod. The six-foot-thick trunks reach a height of 20 to 25 feet before splitting into five or six heavy branches, many of which extend almost straight out horizontally for 50 feet or more.

The house was built in 1971 by two boatbuilders, Eric Johnson and Steve Oldfather, who used a lot of teak, mahogany, and other marine materials, giving the house the cozy feel of an old cabin cruiser. The rough beams underneath are not attached to the tree but slide between pairs of $^3/_4$-inch stainless steel pins driven into the limbs on which the beams rest. This allows the structure to move with the tree.

Linda's partner, Mark, is now planning a second treehouse with curved, laminated redwood rafters, a greenhouse-grade plastic roof, and an ingenious new spiral staircase. The staircase is constructed in sections eight feet high and four feet square that can be stacked on top of each other to attain soaring heights. Each section uses only one and a half sheets of $^3/_4$-inch plywood and four eight-foot two-by-fours.

During February and March the monkeypod tree loses its leaves, and the view is even more spectacular.

The 10-by-20-foot house has a living and sleeping area, a dining area, and a small kitchen, all with beautiful built-in shelves and cabinets. The wall-to-wall windows look out on the valley and a thousand-foot waterfall, which Linda calls the Show. If conditions are right, you can hear the faint thunder of the crashing surf in the distance.

One of the huge branches of the monkeypod tree erupts directly through the floor and divides the bedroom from the kitchen. The kitchen has a sink, cold running water piped in by gravity from the nearby waterfall, an electric stove, and a solar-powered refrigerator. There is a barbecue on the landing outside. For hot showers there is a bathhouse a two-minute walk from the treehouse. Although guests are asked to bring their own food, Linda will provide a picnic basket at a reasonable price.

John Cole, a 29-year-old artist, has built the sturdiest treehouse I have ever seen. It is constructed in post and beam fashion, with earthquake brackets at the top and bottom of every post. A $3/4$-inch cable wraps tightly around the perimeter of the structure at a height of seven feet. A variety of hardwoods were used, including redwood, spruce, pine, fir, and ohea, a native Hawaiian hardwood. Solar panels on the roof provide electrical power for lights and basic appliances. The house is pentagonal in shape, designed to fit into an existing space within a grove of five mango trees on the southeast coast of Hawaii.

John Cole relaxes on the deck of his treehouse, listening to the Pacific Ocean pounding against the jagged basalt cliffs a few yards away.

This abandoned treehouse overlooking a lake in western Washington was once used as a study and diving platform. Now the floor is rotted out, but the owner plans to renovate the house.

Howard Cooper has spent the last 40 years creating his own private botanical garden on 60 acres in a remote part of the Hawaiian island of Maui. In 1957, he planted a banyan tree that in only three decades grew large enough to support a three-story treehouse. He and a friend spent six months of weekends constructing the upper story, then worked their way down to the ground. In the five years since the house was completed, the posts and beams of the substructure have become thoroughly entwined in the branches of the tree. Tree and treehouse are rapidly becoming one.

A rear view of the upper story. To the left is the 12-foot-square bedroom, with a peaked roof and three-foot deck. To the right is the bathroom, with a shed roof. Three eight-inch posts support the back beam of the upper story, while the front beam rests on the tree at three points. The floor joists are two-by-eights, and a truss system made of four-by-fours supports the deck. The middle story is a partially enclosed mezzanine with a kitchen, a few beds, and a covered patio that overlooks the garden and the

Pacific Ocean beyond. Below the mezzanine on the downhill side of the tree is a bunkhouse that was added recently. The camouflage paint is intended to make the house seem more a part of the tree.

A passageway through the twisting boughs of the banyan tree leads to a deck with a spectacular view of a green pasture sloping down to the sea. Near the treehouse Cooper has posted a sign reading, "This is the spot where heaven touches the earth."

When the progressive Pilchuck School opened in 1971 in Bryant, Washington, the students were asked, as an informal part of the curriculum, to build their own housing on the school grounds. Many of the houses still survive, including this treehouse built by Buster Simpson on top of a large cedar stump. The route to the treehouse is as picturesque as the house itself. From the school's woodsy main buildings, you follow a small footpath across a gravel road, past a pond, into a cedar forest, and across a log bridge that spans a gurgling brook. The house is set against the forest just beyond the brook. Buster was working with leftover materials, and old windows were apparently plentiful. But Pilchuck is a glass-blowing school, and it may be that his liberal use of windows reflects an interest in the material. The courtyard behind the house is strewn with discarded glass projects left behind by previous residents.

When Buster accidentally kicked out a window pane during his sleep, he replaced it with a piece of stained glass (lower right corner). Pilchuck students still live in the house.

Building a treehouse on an existing stump is one thing, but I can't say I approve of cutting down a tree in order to create a stump foundation for a treehouse. However, the result in this case is a delightful house, and the view of Mount Rainier is spectacular.

Eric Gains's remarkable two-level treehouse is perched 60 feet up a ponderosa pine on Bly Mountain in south-central Oregon. Like many other arboreal architects, Eric built his house on the ground and hoisted it into position, using a block and tackle and some old mountain climbing gear. He actually built much of the treehouse in San Diego and transported it in his pickup to Oregon, where he spend three weeks assembling it. He has plans to expand to three other trees. To reach the house, you first have to climb 45 feet up an old radio transmission tower attached to the side of the spruce. Then you scramble the last 15 feet on the limbs of the tree and clamber through an opening onto the lower deck. A couple of more limbs and you can crawl through the triangular trap door into the enclosed upper level. The entire structure is supported by a bolt that passes through the tree and the main support beams, and by $1/4$-inch cables running from the ends of the beams to attachment points high on the trunk of the tree. The house is stabilized by additional cables connected to neighboring trees.

Although the house may resemble a flying saucer that has landed in the treetops, it is actually modeled on a traditional Mongol yurt, and living conditions are more reminiscent of the frontier than the space age: water has to be carried up, chamber pots carried down, kerosene lanterns are used for light, and a small gas camping stove provides a little heat. The house is constructed primarily of two-by-sixes, plywood, and Plexiglas, as well as some teak Eric salvaged from old restaurant tables. In addition to the triangular door, there are two closets built into the floor.

Eric was searching for a sense of peace and freedom when he built his house, and he seems to have found it. He is not a recluse, however, and asked if I knew any young women who might be interested in treehouse living.

Michael Garnier's unusual resort, set on 40 acres in the beautiful valley of Takilma, Oregon, offers horseback riding and swimming, but the real attraction is the three treehouses. Michael, who grew up in Gary, Indiana, is a former college wrestler and Green Beret medic who moved to Takilma 20 years ago to help start a medical clinic. After building several conventional guest cabins for his bed-and-breakfast, he completed the first treehouse three years ago. It is perched 20 feet up a sturdy Oregon white oak. The white oaks of western Oregon are notoriously tough trees and thus ideal for treehouses. Michael showed me one that had been strangled by a wire fence that would have killed most other species, but the oak was in apparently good health. Instead of the floating foundation used on many treehouses, Michael decided to build a fixed foundation, attaching a very strong platform firmly to several tree trunks. A fixed platform runs a greater risk of being damaged in a windstorm, but with properly sized beams and connecting hardware, the risk can be greatly reduced. Michael used heavy wooden poles for his beams and floor joists, and he used short sections of channel iron to bolt his main support beams to the tree trunks. The channel iron strengthens the connection between tree and platform, and it reduces the chances of rot by preventing wood-to-wood contact. As often happens with treehouses, Michael built the house first and then thought about the stairs — which ended up costing as much as the house itself. Two smaller treehouses were added later.

The interior of the main house is reminiscent of an old Adirondack lodge. The cedar beadboard on the walls and the fir trim have been oiled and polished until they glow. The comfortable furnishings include a large feather bed, an old-fashioned wall sink, a gilt-edged mirror, and a chamber pot.

Michael recently completed the two smaller treehouses, designed primarily as children's quarters. They are connected by a rope bridge.

Inspired by the geodesic domes of Buckminster Fuller, Ian Christoph and his friend Matt Darrieu built this spectacular treehouse when they were still in high school. It must be one of the few buildings of any sort with a geodesic dome on both top and bottom. First, Ian and Matt built a 12-foot-diameter dome on the ground, then they rolled it over, hoisted it into the trees, and suspended it from three cables. They constructed the spacious deck next, and then completed the upper dome and built a floor inside. Alas, the house is no longer: when the owner of the land discovered it, he had it taken down. Now a master carpenter in California, Ian hopes to recreate his treehouse some day, but perhaps not with a full double dome.

Supported by cables, Ian Christoph's treehouse
seems to float in the air like some unearthly cocoon
or spaceship.

An old cedar stump in Washington state has been turned into an outhouse for a treehouse. The notch on the right side of the stump, level with the door, is where the loggers put the springboards on which they stood while sawing.

A treehouse does not have to be high off the ground to become the favorite place for youngsters. A Washington doctor built this for his young son, carefully crafting openings in the shingled wall for branches.